The Waste Land 1972

Helen Gardner

The Waste Land 1972

The Adamson lecture, 3rd May 1972
University of Manchester

Manchester University Press

© 1972 Manchester University Press

Published by the University of Manchester
at the University Press
316-24 Oxford Road, Manchester M13 9NR

ISBN 0 7190 0540 X

Printed in Great Britain at the St. Ann's Press,
Park Road, Altrincham, Cheshire WA14 5QQ.

The Waste Land in 1972 is a different poem from the poem that was printed in October 1922 in *The Criterion*. The words on the page are the same, but their meaning is different. In a very obvious way, it is no longer a bold and strange experiment, something new and exciting, which we meet with no preconceptions and encounter with a certain bafflement. It is familiar. Even those who read it for the first time cannot quite read it in the same way 'for the first time' as its first readers did. They come to it conscious of its fame. Then, also, it has changed, as all historic objects change as they become a part of history. It is now clearly a poem written at a certain time, at a certain period of history as well as at a certain period of literary history. The circumstances in which it was written we have to recover by an effort of memory or imagination. It is a 'post-war' poem, but not a 'post-any-war' poem; it is a poem of the early 'twenties, of the years immediately following the first world war. It has also changed in a profounder way, by becoming what fifty years of reading and absorption into the minds and imaginations of its readers have made of it. It is a poem which has been lived with, enriched and given new resonances by the life-experiences of its readers, and by the discussion it has aroused, by the questions asked of it, and the answers given, by its critics and its lovers. An enormous literature has grown up around it, some brilliantly helpful, some, we may feel, an exercise in obfuscation, some tedious and trivial, and some plainly wrong-headed; but even what we may reject or regard as useless has played some part in creating *The Waste Land* of 1972. All this discussion and interpretation has entered our minds, the minds that receive the poem again on each re-reading. Although each time we read it properly it gives us a fresh experience, that fresh experience is the heir of past experiences, of memories of earlier readings, of knowledge of many kinds gained over the years.

It is also a different poem because we now read it not only in the light of what went before but in the light of what came after. To its first readers it was the striking new poem by the author of *Prufrock*, the *Preludes*, the Sweeney poems, and *Gerontion*. To us it is also the poem of the poet who was to write *The Hollow Men*, *Ash Wednesday*, the Ariel poems, *Murder in the Cathedral*, *The Family Reunion* and *Four Quartets*. It was, when it appeared, the peak of Eliot's achievement: the culmination of his earlier poetry. It is now a peak in a whole landscape with which we are familiar: the landscape of Eliot's mind and sensibility as revealed in his completed work. We interpret it by what comes after as well as by what went before; and this is true even if we feel, as some do, that it remains the peak, and that the later work does not reach to its height. I have sometimes played with the idea of annotating Eliot purely by Eliot, and substituting for the notes he provided for *The Waste Land* annotations from his own work. Certainly, to me, both *The Family Reunion* and *Four Quartets* enormously clarify and enrich my reading of *The Waste Land*.

Eliot himself said that a poet can try

> to give an honest report of the way in which he himself writes . . . And in one sense, but a very limited one, he knows better what his poems "mean" than can anyone else; he may know the history of their composition, the material which has gone in and come out in unrecognisable form, and he knows what he was trying to do and what he was meaning to mean. But what a poem means is as much what it means to others as what it means to the author; and indeed, in the course of time a poet may become merely a reader in respect to his own works, forgetting his original meaning—or without forgetting, merely changing.[1]

Eliot was commenting on I. A. Richards's statement that *The Waste Land* effects 'a complete severance between poetry and *all* beliefs'. And he declared that as a reader of his poem he was no better qualified to say 'No!' than any other reader, though he added his own opinion, *qua* reader and not *qua* author, that 'either Mr Richards is wrong, or I do not understand his meaning'. Eliot was playing with the question of what

1 *The Use of Poetry and the Use of Criticism* (1933), 130.

is meant by 'meaning'. His statement does not give a licence to any reader, sensitive or otherwise, to interpret the sense of a poem as he chooses, or to speculate on the biographical significance of incidents and feelings in it, or to insist that this was what the author 'really meant', whatever he declared he meant to mean, and this is what he was really trying to do. He was attempting to defend the integrity of a poem against those who would extract from it some neat summation as its meaning, or those who expect poets to tell them what their poems mean. He rightly saw that Richards's statement was a statement of the poem's effect, not of its intention, and countered by saying he thought this was either wrong— presumably meaning that 'this is not its effect on me as I read it'—or nonsense. One wishes he had gone a little further in his role as reader, not author, of his own poem, and tried to show Richards why his response was wrong. But, alas, as so often with Eliot's criticism, he stops just when one wishes he would go on. Presumably he would have argued that Richards, though a sensitive reader, was being insensitive to some elements in the poem and therefore was not receiving its full effect.

Certain attempts to find the meaning of *The Waste Land* Eliot reacted against—it would seem, on two grounds: that they were false to what he 'meant to mean' and was 'trying to do' when he wrote the poem, and that they seemed, like Richards's statement, to provide a limiting cliché for the poem's effect or meaning. He plainly felt that Richards's statement that the poem effected a severance between poetry and all beliefs confused dogmas with beliefs, and ignored the poem's religious dimension, 'the specifically religious theme in its orchestration', as Dr Leavis called it, its strong impulse towards asceticism and discipline, which are belief in action, and all the implications of its central theme of man's need for rebirth. He also, and on more than one occasion, queried or mocked at those who saw the poem as of mainly contemporary relevance: 'the expression of the disillusion of a generation'.

4

Mrs Eliot has put as preface to the facsimile one such denial of sociological intention:

> Various critics have done me the honour to interpret the poem in terms of criticism of the contemporary world, have considered it, indeed, as an important bit of social criticism. To me it was only the relief of a personal and wholly insignificant grouse against life; it is just a piece of rhythmical grumbling.

Some people have expressed uneasiness to me at the prominence given to this sentence from a lecture, which might be read as the remark of a poet rather dishonestly denigrating his own work. But Eliot is here speaking of what he knows: of what he intended. He had not intended his poem as a piece of social criticism: he knew its origins were deeply personal. He speaks of the personal pain from which it sprang in ironically denigratory terms as unimportant in the great scheme of things—not like the Great War, or the Russian revolution, or the collapse of the Austrian Empire, or the decline of religious belief, or all the other great events and great movements that readers have seen as contributory to *The Waste Land* and reflected in it. Eliot was not saying that the poem cannot be read in this way—only that this was not his intention. His poem was written in accordance with his theory of poetry—a theory born, like all the critical theories of poets, from knowledge of his own practice. He wrote it as the relief for, and as the objectification of, 'a complex tissue of feelings and desires' and deep and obscure emotions.[1] There is irony in calling these an 'insignificant grouse against life', as if this aim of dragging into the light and objectifying the sources of one's profoundest feelings were less important than writing social criticism; and there was also the protectiveness that Eliot, for obvious reasons, always displayed on the subject of his first marriage. But fundamentally he was directing readers back to the poem, away from what it had been said to 'mean'.

1 'Ben Jonson', in *Selected Essays, 1917-1932* (1932), 158.

Better to listen to it as a 'piece of rhythmical grumbling' than
to use it as a criticism of life in London in 1922.

In the notorious essay on *Hamlet* in 1919, when Eliot
declared the play to be an artistic failure, because Shakespeare
'had tackled a problem which proved too much for him',
he ended by saying:

> Why he attempted it at all is an insoluble puzzle; under
> compulsion of what experience he attempted to express the
> inexpressibly horrible, we cannot ever know. We need a great
> many facts in his biography; and we should like to know
> whether, and when, and after or at the same time as what personal
> experience, he read Montaigne, II. xii, *Apologie de Raimond
> Sebond*. We should have, finally, to know something which is
> by hypothesis unknowable, for we assume it to be an experi-
> ence which, in the manner indicated, exceeded the facts. We
> should have to understand, things which Shakespeare did not
> understand himself.[1]

Eliot allows here for the importance of knowing biographical
facts, and of the relation of these to literary sources. But
in the last sentence, and earlier in the paragraph, he hints
at their comparative unimportance, speaking of 'the intense
feeling, ecstatic or terrible, without an object, or exceeding
its object' as something which every person of sensibility
has known, adding that the 'ordinary person puts these feelings
to sleep, or trims down his feelings to fit the business world;
the artist keeps them alive by his ability to intensify the world
to his emotions.' In one sense we can say that *The Waste Land*
is the product of Eliot's unhappy first marriage, and, to use
his own words, that it was under the 'compulsion' of this
experience that he 'attempted to express the inexpressibly
horrible'. We can also say that reading Miss Weston's book
From Ritual to Romance, published in 1920, with its demon-
stration of the inextricable knot that ties the twin mysteries
of sex and religion, precipitated the final form of the poem he

1 *Selected Essays, 1917-1932,* 146.

had meditated writing. But neither post-war disillusion, nor the reading of Miss Weston's book, nor his failure to find or to give happiness in marriage, explain *The Waste Land* or give us its meaning, though they can all give us approaches to its meaning.

Although it was not the poet's intention, *The Waste Land* voices the despairing sense that Europe had committed suicide in the 1914–18 war. In reading it we recapture a mood and a tone that is unlike the post-war mood of the late 1940's: the sense of an appalling catastrophe that had not merely destroyed what was beautiful but had revealed it as a sham. Pound expressed this explicitly in *Hugh Selwyn Mauberley*:

> There died a myriad,
> And of the best, among them,
> For an old bitch gone in the teeth,
> For a botched civilisation,

and

> Died some, pro patria, 'non dulce' non 'et decor' . . .
> walked eye-deep in hell
> believing in old men's lies, then unbelieving
> came home, home to a lie,
> home to many deceits,
> home to old lies and new infamy.

Less explicitly than this, lines such as

> What are the roots that clutch, what branches grow
> Out of this stony rubbish?

met and gave an image for the same sense of living in the *detritus* of a civilisation, among a 'heap of broken images'. The vision of 'crowds of people, walking round in a ring', of the crowds flowing over London Bridge, 'And each man fixed his eyes before his feet', which culminates in

> hooded hordes swarming
> Over endless plains, stumbling in cracked earth
> Ringed by the flat horizon only

conveys a deep sense of meaninglessness, of human beings reduced to automata, and at last to swarming, faceless creatures, driven by the animal urge to survive, famished and animated by a mass terror. Eliot was entitled to deny that he intended to express the disillusion of a generation, that his poem was intended to be topical; but it is topical. It expresses a sense of having come, as it were, to the end of a road, of decay, of lack of any sense of purpose. It gives us, to employ the title of a work he quoted in the notes, a *Blick ins Chaos*. He did, after all, in his note to Part V, specify the 'decay of Eastern Europe' as one of its three themes. In the little vignette of a party drinking coffee in the Hofgarten of the Residenz at Munich before the war, the lady who declares so proudly that she isn't Russian but a true-blue German, though she comes from Lithuania, must have made some of the poem's first readers wonder what had happened to her in the confusions out of which the now defunct Baltic States emerged at Versailles. And Marie's cousin, the archduke, who took her out in a sled, was he the same archduke who was shot at Sarajevo? Both women are speaking from a once static world, now gone. In 1922 in impoverished Austria there were no archdukes in their castles to take their little cousins out sledding. And Mr Eugenides, the Greek merchant from Smyrna, arouses questions too. At this time the Greek populations of Asia Minor were menaced by the revival of Turkey, and the Near East was in ferment with the rash and fatal Greek invasion of Anatolia. Only a year after *The Waste Land* was published, Smyrna was to go up in flames and its large Greek population was to be deported. The sense that 'History is now and London' is a note that recurs through *The Waste Land*, though London, like other cities, is an 'Unreal City' and the waste land itself is timeless and unlocalised, a state and not a place.

As for the sources, Eliot, in his lecture on 'The Frontiers of Criticism',[1] referred ruefully to the famous notes, explaining that he had provided them in response to the request of his

1 *On Poetry and Poets* (1957), 109-10.

American publisher, who thought the poem itself was too short to fill up the whole volume. This was the origin, he explained, of what he described as a 'remarkable exposition of bogus scholarship'. He added that although it was just for him to pay tribute to Miss Weston's book, he regretted that he had 'sent so many enquirers off on a wild goose chase after Tarot cards and the Holy Grail'. Even without this warning, I think it is clear that attempts to find an organisation of the poem by relating it to any version of the Grail story are misleading, and that continual references to the Fisher King, the Quester or Deliverer, and the Grail Maiden distort the separate episodes, and are an attempt to impose a meaning on the poem that it cannot bear, and which destroys the meaning which it has. They lead often to a kind of censorious moralising that is quite alien to the poem's moral feeling, as each supposed 'Quester' is censured for his 'failure'. Thus the beauty of the Phlebas lyric, with its mingled note of envy and grief, is destroyed by seeing Phlebas as only another potential Deliverer who has failed in his task. We have been told by one critic that he is 'a soul lost through routine and unimaginative desires. Phlebas has his finer side, when he listens to the gulls and the sea, but his directing principle is "profit and loss" and this is his ruin.' Oh dear! Do indifference to material concerns, and listening to seagulls, protect against shipwreck? And the same critic sounds the same severe note in dealing with the various women, who are 'aspects of the one Woman who should help the Deliverer to break the curse of impotence in the waste land'.

> 'My feet are at Moorgate, and my heart
> Under my feet. After the event
> He wept. He promised "a new start."
> I made no comment. What should I resent?'

This, we are told, is 'callous in its lack of remorse, and shows how the woman is impervious to the emotional reactions of the

man'.[1] The figures in *The Waste Land*, voices heard in a
briefly sketched setting, or figures caught in some significant
act, resist this kind of treatment. They cannot be 'placed'
as if they were characters in a novel. And the progress of the
poem to its conclusion is not a narrative progress. It even
seems wrong to speak of there being a narrator in this poem.

It has been wittily said that while Miss Weston called her
book *From Ritual to Romance*, Eliot might have subtitled his
poem 'From Romance to Ritual'. What fired his imagination
was not the Grail story in any of its versions, but what Miss
Weston declared lay behind the romances: the myth of a land
made waste by the sickness of its ruler, waiting for a deliverer.
This she related to other myths of death and rebirth, expressive
of the cycle of aridity and fertility in nature and in man;
myths of deaths and resurrections of gods who were life-
bringers: slain gods and buried gods, or drowned gods,
passionately mourned by wailing women, and rapturously
greeted on their return or resurrection, when new life returned
to the land and to beasts and men with the rising of the waters
or the coming of the rain. In all these myths, the 'knot
intrinsecate' between sex and religion was expressed, the
intimate bond between man's physical and his spiritual nature;
and all implied that new life must be born out of suffering and
death as winter must precede spring. In some details Miss
Weston's book is illuminating. It explains, perhaps, the presence
of the Tarot cards in the poem; for she tells us they were used
to foretell the rising and falling of the waters. But although
this may explain the presence of the Tarot pack, it does not
help us to see what Eliot has made of it, or to interpret the
prophecies of Madame Sosostris snuffling through her cold.

1 Quotations are from the late Sir Maurice Bowra's essay on T. S. Eliot in
  The Creative Experiment (1949), 163-88. This is the most thoroughgoing
  attempt to 'extract its framework from *The Waste Land*' and find behind
  all its characters and scenes the 'main figures of the Grail Ritual, the
  Fisher King, who embodies the sterility of the land, the Deliverer, whose
  task is to break the curse, and the Woman with whom he breaks it'.

To attempt to impose on the episodes of *The Waste Land* the figures of the Grail myth is to substitute for what the poem gives us an essentially reductive scheme. We are imposing on the poem terms it does not use. 'The Quester' or 'the Deliverer', and 'the Grail Maiden' are not present in the poem. Nor, for that matter, does the Fisher King appear in the final version any more than he did in the first draft. Pound ringed, in Madame Sosostris's 'Here is the man with three staves', the words 'man with three staves' in Eliot's typescript, and Eliot wrote above it 'King fishing', and then cancelled this for 'fisher King'. But he thought better of this, and reverted in the poem he published to his first inspiration: the enigmatic 'man with three staves'. The Fisher King, with his wound, is behind, not within the poem. In the poem we have only the image of a man fishing. It does not occur until the third section:

> While I was fishing in the dull canal
> On a winter evening round behind the gashouse.

The canal and the gasworks were spotted by Poldy Bloom on his way to Paddy Dignam's funeral, where, as the carriage he was riding in jolted over the street, he remembered an old rhyme:

> Rattle her bones
> Over the stones,
> Only a pauper
> Whom nobody owns.

'The rattle of the bones and the chuckle spread from ear to ear', the Cheshire cat's grin made audible; the footman's snicker in *Prufrock* coarsened into an eerie chuckle—these introduce the man fishing. He is the wounded king of legend, but he is also Ferdinand, Prince of Naples, musing on the deaths of kings in shipwreck, but more than this he is primarily an urban image of solitude, passivity, and waiting. What a melancholy image this is: a solitary huddled figure fishing in these unprofitable waters, seen in the back streets of a town.

It might come out of a novel by Simenon, who was to be one of Eliot's favourite authors. Fishing in a dull canal on a winter's evening round behind the gashouse does seem an archetypal hopeless enterprise. This image of a man fishing is picked up again at the close of the poem:

> I sat upon the shore
> Fishing, with the arid plain behind me

This second occurrence of the image, with the whole poem behind it, has overtones. Eliot himself referred us in the last section to the journey to Emmaus, so it is perhaps not illicit to remember here the last chapter of St John's Gospel, when Peter went a-fishing. And here the man sits by a great river or a lake or the sea, with 'the arid plains behind him'. It is a different image from the dreary image of a man fishing in the dull canal on a winter evening round behind the gashouse.

Eliot provided another clue, which has also, I think, proved a snare and a false light, in his note on Tiresias and his long quotation from Ovid's *Metamorphoses*.

> Tiresias, although a mere spectator, and not indeed a 'character', is yet the most important personage in the poem, uniting all the rest. Just as the one-eyed merchant, seller of currants, melts into the Phoenician sailor, and the latter is not wholly distinct from Ferdinand Prince of Naples, so all the women are one woman, and the two sexes meet in Tiresias. What Tiresias *sees*, in fact, is the substance of the poem.

This note, intended to warn us that there are no 'characters' in *The Waste Land*, has led, like the desire to identify the Fisher King, the Quester, and the Grail Maiden, to the most extraordinary exegetical feats, in which Tiresias is turned into a kind of hero of the poem and endures the most extraordinary metamorphoses, as if Eliot had said 'What Tiresias *does*, or remembers having done' was the substance of the poem, and the poem was the reminiscences of a quick-change artist, perpetually changing his sex. Tiresias, like the man fishing, does not appear until the centre of the poem, at the beginning and the close of the episode of the typist and the house-agent's clerk. Having appeared there, he never appears again. He is Poet and Seer. I suspect that he first came into the poem more from the *Odyssey* than from Ovid, and from the *Odyssey* via the first three cantos of Pound's *Cantos*, and that Eliot, writing in an age more familiar with the classics than ours, assumed that the Tiresias of Sophocles, the Theban seer, burdened with knowledge that is of no avail, taunted by Oedipus with blindness, but who has seen the past, understands the present, and foresees the future, and the Tiresias whom Osysseus met in Hades, was the Tiresias that his readers, without the notes he later supplied, would recognise appearing at the poem's centre. He appears at the heart of 'The Fire Sermon', where the theme is lust. The passage from Ovid, supplied in the notes, explains his appearance there. He had offended the deities of generation by striking two great snakes that he saw coupling, and was changed to a woman; but after seven years he saw them again, and struck again, and was restored to his former sex. Having experienced the act of sex as both man and woman, he appears at the climactic centre of the poem, knowing all, foreseeing all, understanding all: 'Old man with wrinkled dugs'. He has

> sat by Thebes below the wall
And walked among the lowest of the dead.

Now, in London in the typist's bed-sitter, he awaits 'the expected guest'. His vision, we are told, is the poem: all are included in it, the barbarous King and his victim changed into the bird that sings yet so doth wail, the ravished nightingale, the young man and the typist in their bored and boring copulation, the Lady of Situations and her silent husband, the hyacinth girl, the fortune-teller peering into the future—all male and female who pass before us, melting and merging into each other, creatures of memory and imagination and observation, of a uniting consciousness in which they live and play their parts. He is the consciousness of the poet made visible for a short space in the centre of the poem in mythical form. The progression is clear from J. Alfred Prufrock, through Gerontion, to Tiresias. Prufrock has some kind of fictional identity, and is firmly set in time and place. The little old man of 'Gerontion', in his decayed, windy house, is presented to us at the opening of the poem as a dominant image that recurs, and his image closes the poem too. Though he is not in any sense a 'character' he is a focus for all the feelings and memories of the poem, an image that haunts us of old age, of life reduced to thoughts endlessly churning round: 'Thoughts of a dry brain in a dry season'. There is no such dominating image in *The Waste Land*. Tiresias, who emerges for a moment at the poem's centre, who is of every time and no time, male and female, blind yet gifted with special sight, who knows that there is nothing new under the sun, and that all places are one place and all times one time, is type of the poet-prophet. He is one of those whom Milton evoked:

Blind Thamyris and blind Maeonides
And Tiresias and Phineus, prophets old.

His presence and the note on him tell us that this is a visionary poem, and a prophetic poem. He gives authority to its urgent commands.

Other myths are built into the poem, combining with, and superimposed on, its flashes of vivid actuality: the myth of Philomela—the nightingale who 'sings of adulterous wrong'— the myth of *The Tempest*, of Ferdinand, Prince of Naples, who mourns for deaths by water, cast by shipwreck upon a strange isle where music steals upon the waters. It has recently been suggested that the poem owes far more than its epigraph to the *Satyricon* of Petronius.[1] And the poem is soaked in echoes and reminiscences of other poems, some obvious, some

[1] See Francis Noel Lees, 'Mr Eliot's Sunday morning *Satura*: Petronius and *The Waste Land*', in *T. S. Eliot: the Man and his Work*, ed. Allen Tate (1966), 345-54.

latent. Conrad Aiken, reviewing *The Waste Land* in *The New Republic* in February 1923, headed his review 'An Anatomy of Melancholy'. He tells us that he told Eliot he had done so, and Eliot turned on him 'with that icy fury of which he alone was capable, and said fiercely: "There is nothing melancholy about it!" ' 'The reference, Tom,' replied Aiken mildly, 'was to Burton's *Anatomy of Melancholy*, and the quite extraordinary amount of *quotation* it contains!'[1] Some of these quotations are obvious: those the poet thought we needed to recognise he kindly identified in the notes. Some are very obscure, and others are echoes, possibly quite unconscious, stored up in Eliot's marvellously retentive brain. How helpful it is to be told in line after line that this is 'possibly a reminiscence of this or that' I have become increasingly doubtful. Does the line describing the typist's combinations as 'Out of the window perilously spread' really 'seem to owe something to Keats's *Ode to a Nightingale*'? And are the monotonous iterations of 'Nothing' in 'A Game of Chess' really 'reminiscent (not without gross overtones) of Lear's warning to Cordelia "Nothing will come of nothing. Speak again." '? The connection and the 'gross overtones' escape me. Since ironic reminiscence and unexpected collocations are characteristic of Eliot's manner and style, almost any verbal coincidence, however far-fetched, can be taken as establishing an ironic parallel or reminiscent debt. On the principle that 'there are salmons in both', almost any line in the poem can be found to be reminiscent, if sufficient concordances are easily available to the exegete. I do not mean to suggest that in a general study of Eliot's poetry the amount of reminiscence, whether conscious or unconscious, is not important; but that such source-hunting does not help us to read *The Waste Land*.

We know now from the drafts that Eliot originally intended to use as the epigraph to his poem a quotation from Conrad's

1 The story is told and the original review reprinted in Conrad Aiken's contribution to Allen Tate's memorial volume referred to above, pp. 194-202.

Heart of Darkness:

> Did he live his life again in every detail of desire, temptation, and surrender during that supreme moment of complete knowledge? He cried in a whisper at some image, at some vision —he cried out twice, a cry that was no more than a breath—
>   'The horror! The horror!'

Pound, in a letter to Eliot, queried the use of this quotation, saying, 'I doubt if Conrad is weighty enough to stand the citation.' And Eliot wrote later from London, asking him to explain his objection: 'Do you mean not use the Conrad quote or simply not put Conrad's name to it? It is much the most appropriate I can find, and somewhat elucidative.' In Conrad's story, Marlow, the narrator, observes of Kurtz, 'The wilderness found him out . . . I think it had whispered to him things about himself which he did not know . . . and the whisper had proved irresistibly fascinating. It echoed loudly within him because he was hollow at the core.' When Eliot said that the Conrad quotation was somewhat elucidative he pointed us very clearly to the major source of *The Waste Land*. It is a report on experience, and it is a report on the experience of a life, and not merely on immediate experience. The immediate circumstances in which the poem was written are clear enough from the letters Mrs Eliot quotes in her introduction and from information which has been available for a very long time. Some years later Eliot attempted to objectify in dramatic form a tragic marriage relation, and in a long letter to Martin Browne, the producer of *The Family Reunion*, he went very far towards explaining the immediate compulsions under which he wrote *The Waste Land*. He was replying to a rather obtuse suggestion that the solution for Harry, the tormented hero who believes he has murdered his wife, would be to marry his young cousin, Mary.

> The point of Mary, in relation to Harry, was meant to be this. The effect of his married life upon him was one of such horror as to leave him for the time at least in a state that may be called

one of being psychologically partially desexed: or rather, it has given him a horror of women as of unclean creatures. The scene with Mary is meant to bring out . . . the conflict inside him between this repulsion for Mary as a woman, and the attraction which the *normal* part of him that is still left, feels towards her personally *for the first time*. This is the first time since his marriage ('there was no ecstacy') that he has been attracted towards any woman.

Later in the same letter Eliot speaks of the 'doubt' as to whether his hero, Harry, had really pushed his wife overboard, or only thought he had.

> Suppose that the desire for her death was strong in his mind, out of touch with reality in her company. He is standing on the deck, perhaps a few feet away, and she is leaning over the rail. She has sometimes talked of suicide. The whole scene of pushing her over—or giving her just a little tip—passes through his mind. She is trying to play one of her comedies with him—to arouse *any* emotion in him is better than to feel that he is not noticing her . . .[1]

It is plain that Harry's wife in *The Family Reunion*, like Belladonna in 'A Game of Chess', was a 'Lady of Situations', whose hysteria and emotional demands on her husband drove him in on himself, inhibiting all desire:

> 'What shall I do now? What shall I do?'
> 'I shall rush out as I am, and walk the street
> 'With my hair down, so.

We can take *The Family Reunion* as a kind of gloss on the second section of *The Waste Land*, and to some extent as elucidatory of the despair and horror at the poem's core. But earlier poetry can be used as a gloss too. Long before his marriage, in 'Portrait of a Lady', and 'Prufrock', and in *La Figlia che Piange*', poems written at Harvard, Eliot had explored failures in human relationships, boredom, ennui, baffled desire, and haunting feelings of guilt. Eliot is from the beginning a

1 E. Martin Browne, *The Making of T. S. Eliot's Plays* (1970), 106-8.

poet of the conscience, and of the burdened conscience, of 'cogitations' that amaze 'The troubled midnight and the noon's repose'. Investigation into a poet's life, even when conducted with sympathy, sensitiveness, and psychological insight, cannot take us very far towards real understanding of a poem and, if it lures us into treating the poem as primarily a document in the poet's biography, can virtually destroy the poem as an imaginative creation. It is plain that all Eliot's poetry is profoundly personal. He is a poet of narrow range; but within that range he goes very deep. Biography can give us often the proximate sources of the personal feeling of a poem; the deeper sources may for ever elude the biographer's search. In an unpublished letter to John Hayward in 1941, replying to his comments on the first draft of 'Little Gidding' Eliot wrote, 'The defect of the whole poem, I feel, is the lack of some acute personal reminiscence (never to be explicated, of course, but to give power from well below the surface).'[1] I do not think by 'an acute personal reminiscence' he necessarily meant the kind of information we find in biographies.

> Why, [he once wrote] . . . out of all that we have heard, seen, felt, in a lifetime, do certain images recur, charged with emotion, rather than others? The song of one bird, the leap of one fish, at a particular place and time, the scent of one flower, an old woman on a German mountain path, six ruffians seen through an open window playing cards at night at a small French railway junction where there was a water-mill: such memories may have symbolic value, but of what we cannot tell, for they come to represent the depths of feeling into which we cannot peer. We might just as well ask why, when we try to recall visually some period in the past, we find in our memory just the few meagre arbitrarily chosen set of snapshots that we do find there, the faded poor souvenirs of passionate moments.[2]

It is in these depths of feeling into which we cannot peer that the true source of the power of *The Waste Land* lies.

1 Quoted with permission of Mrs Valerie Eliot.
2 *The Use of Poetry and the Use of Criticism*, 148.

Some may claim that these depths are accessible in the light of modern knowledge of psychology, and I would agree that the presence of obsessive situations and obsessive images throughout the range of a poet's work provides a real key to some of the deeper levels of a poet's personality. It is a key that needs to be used with great delicacy, but it can unlock doors. It is, however, quite another matter to erect a psychological theory on the basis of a single poem and a few misunderstood biographical facts, and then claim that this theory explains the poem. I must just refer to the hypothesis, rightly described by Professor Ellmann, in reviewing a recent book which revived it, as 'self-defeating', that the source of the distress at the heart of *The Waste Land* was the author's homosexuality. This reached new heights of absurdity in the correspondence columns of the *Times Literary Supplement* following the publication of the drafts of *The Waste Land*. Leaving on one side the fact that to his friends and throughout the whole range of his works Eliot's personality, to use Wyndham Lewis's words, 'visibly moved within the male pale',[1] the theory makes no sense of *The Waste Land* as a whole. The range of feeling of horror and desolation in it, which made Eliot feel the Conrad quotation 'somewhat elucidative', cannot be tied down to the sense of loss for a friend's death, however passionately mourned, and the sense of sick horror and disgust, of terrible boredom, and of the failure of the springs of life and feeling embraces both men and women. If the typist is 'bored and tired', the young man is equally so;

> His vanity requires no response,
> And makes a welcome of indifference.

If the lonely man fishing is an image of solitude, so is the girl among the crowds on Margate Sands who can 'connect nothing with nothing'. It is the whole human condition that arouses horror in *The Waste Land*. And most of all, this reading

1 Wyndham Lewis, 'Early London environment', in *T. S. Eliot: a Symposium*, ed. Richard March and M. J. Tambimuttu (1948), 251.

of the poem takes no account of the final section, the poem's crown and completion.

I seem so far to have been rather negative and to have been largely occupied in suggesting ways not to read *The Waste Land*. But I hope there has been emerging, if not suggestions as to *the* way to read *The Waste Land*, at least some hints as to how I read it. Its best critics, beginning with Eliot's undergraduate friend and fellow poet Conrad Aiken, have always insisted on a musical analogy. 'We "accept" the poem,' wrote Aiken, 'as we would accept a powerful, melancholy tone-poem.' He put the word 'accept' in inverted commas, and rightly, for the secret of the meaning of *The Waste Land* is only open to those who will accept it for what it is, and not tease it into conformity with some plan. It is not a cryptogram to be solved but a poem to be listened to. 'Its parts,' said Aiken in the same review, 'are not important parts of an important or careful intellectual pattern; but they are important parts of an important emotional ensemble.' The relation between them is 'a dim and tonal one, not exact'. Aiken even went so far as to regret Eliot's attempt to unify by interweaving and repetition of phrases and images, referring to them as giving the poem a 'spurious but happy sequence' whose value is that it creates a 'necessary superficial formal unity'. This goes too far, but it is an error in the right direction. *The Waste Land* demands, in the first place, the strongest possible immediate response, however violent the extremes of response demanded from moment to moment. It was created out of disparate experiences that came to cohere for the poet. Its individual readers have to find what coherence it has for them. No critic can provide them with a magic thread to take them through the labyrinth. Its connections are not connections of logic, but connections of feeling, often of violent reactions of feeling. Through the years it has come to me to have an extraordinary tone of authority. This is achieved by the energy of its language, and the vitality of its varying rhythms. It lives in the memory in marvellous lines and powerful rhythms. As I read it I feel myself being directed or played on by a master who obtains his effects without any hesitation or fumbling, who asks only that I should let my heart beat in accordance with his controlling hands. Partly this is achieved by the modulation between 'I' and 'We', which continually draws us into the poem. There is no poem in which the reader is more involved. It is a poem that makes the reader work hard.

It begins authoritatively with a bold paradox stated as fact, something incontrovertible: 'April is the cruellest month'. It can command us:

(Come in under the shadow of this red rock),
And I will show you something different from either
Your shadow at morning striding behind you
Or your shadow at evening rising to meet you;
I will show you fear in a handful of dust.

It breaks with sudden dramatic intensity into the vision it imposes on us of a city of the dead, with a voice that is bold and sardonic:

Unreal City,
Under the brown fog of a winter dawn,
A crowd flowed over London Bridge, so many,
I had not thought death had undone so many.
Sighs, short and infrequent, were exhaled,
And each man fixed his eyes before his feet.
Flowed up the hill and down King William Street,
To where Saint Mary Woolnoth kept the hours
With a dead sound on the final stroke of nine.
There I saw one I knew, and stopped him, crying: 'Stetson!
'You who were with me in the ships at Mylae!
'That corpse you planted last year in your garden,
'Has it begun to sprout? Will it bloom this year?
'Or has the sudden frost disturbed its bed?
'Oh keep the Dog far hence, that's friend to men,
'Or with his nails he'll dig it up again!
'You! hypocrite lecteur!—mon semblable,—mon frère!'

There is first the distant view which we see as outsiders, then
we are in the crowd and there is the sudden arrest and questions,
and last it is *we* who are being addressed. 'Has it begun to
sprout? Will it *bloom* this year?' The intellectual vivacity that
provides these unexpected verbs demands a responding
vivacity from us. So do the sudden collocations of totally
disparate feelings in such a passage as

> But at my back from time to time I hear
> The sound of horns and motors, which shall bring
> Sweeney to Mrs Porter in the spring.
> O the moon shone bright on Mrs Porter
> And on her daughter
> They wash their feet in soda water
> *Et O ces voix d'enfants, chantant dans la coupole!*

The note refers us to Verlaine's sonnet '*Parsifal*'. The association
of ideas may well be through Mrs Porter and her daughter
washing their hot, tired feet, through the ritual washing of
feet in Wagner's *Parsifal* to Verlaine's sonnet; but the *effect*
in the poem, after the rattle of bones and the fisherman on a
winter evening by the dull canal, and Ferdinand mourning
the death of kings, and naked bodies cast up on the shore,
and bones in a garret, rattled by rats' feet, and the premonition
of a spring which will only bring together Sweeney and
Mrs Porter, is of an extraordinary sense of relief and refresh-
ment at hearing the sexless, unearthly voices of children
echoing in a high dome. It is a sudden intimation of a world of
purity and innocence.

The same effect is given on a larger scale by the lyrical
'Death by Water' coming after the close of 'The Fire Sermon':

> Burning burning burning burning
> O Lord Thou pluckest me out
> O Lord Thou pluckest
>
> burning
>
> Phlebas the Phoenician, a fortnight dead,
> Forgot the cry of gulls, and the deep sea swell

And the profit and loss.
                    A current under sea
Picked his bones in whispers. As he rose and fell
He passed the stages of his age and youth
Entering the whirlpool.
                    Gentile or Jew
O you who turn the wheel and look to windward,
Consider Phlebas, who was once handsome and tall as you.

If Eliot had provided epigraphs from Dickens for all the sections of *The Waste Land*, he might well have put above 'Death by Water' the remark of Dismal Jimmy in the fifth chapter of *The Pickwick Papers*, which so surprised Mr Pickwick: 'Did it ever strike you, on such a morning as this, that drowning would be happiness and peace?' There is no fear of death in this lyric, as in 'a handful of dust', and there is none of the macabre feeling of bones in a garret rattled by the rat's foot, or of crabs crawling over a stomach and eels growing grossly fat eating drowned flesh as in a little fragment and the Dirge for Bleistein printed in the drafts. Here it is the deep currents of the sea that have 'picked his bones in whispers'. Phlebas has forgotten both happiness and anxiety, the calculations of daily life, he has passed backwards through the stages of his life into a primal innocence, cleanness and nothingness, back into the waters in which we lay before birth. The final admonition has an austere gentleness and sweetness. The interpretation of 'Death by Water' is helped by our knowledge of the preceding passages that Eliot cancelled. Though Pound may have been right in denouncing the three quatrains on the sailor as 'Bad', they give us Eliot's feeling about those 'who turn the wheel and look to windward': that their commerce with the sea makes them retain 'Something inhuman, clean and dignified'. 'Death by Water' is clean. Coming before the last section of the poem, it washes the imagination free of Sweeney and Mrs Porter, and the typist and the young man, of Elizabeth and Leicester, of 'Trams and dusty trees', and feet tramping the pavements at Moorgate, and 'The broken fingernails of dirty hands', and of Carthage, 'cauldron of unholy lusts'. The theme of lust disappears from the poem, as do disgust and loathing. When fire returns at the end it is another fire: the fire which refines.

Although I feel that the attempt to impose plot on *The Waste Land* wrongs it, I cannot agree with those who do not find in it progress, and a conclusion that, although open-ended, is a true conclusion. The titles of the sections guide us. 'The Burial of the Dead': but the dead will not stay buried. We are creatures of memory, and memory arouses desire. The power of the past, the hopes and fears of the future, make the present unbearable, a desert.

> Men's curiosity searches past and future
> And clings to that dimension.[1]

The past—in the sunlight in the Hofgarten, and coming back from the hyacinth garden; the future—into which Madame Sosostris peers with her wicked pack of cards; the present—in the desert, or flowing over London Bridge. In both these last there comes a moment of arrest: 'fear in a handful of dust', 'the corpse you planted last year in your garden'. The second section is the simplest. It is all in the present, and the dramatic present. It was originally to be called 'In the Cage'; for the title 'A Game of Chess' Eliot referred us to *Women Beware Women*. I have never quite seen the point of the allusion, and the title has rather lost by Eliot's excision at his wife's request of the line 'The ivory men make company between us'. But without Middleton's play to help or hinder, the title seems to have point enough. As one of Congreve's heroines remarked, if love is a game one of the players must be a loser. A game of chess always ends in mating, but the mating is either checkmate, one player being the loser, or stalemate, when both players lose, or fool's mate. This is the most limited section of the poem, the least evocative. 'Time' here is a meaningless succession of moments which will be arrested by a knock

1 'The Dry Salvages'.

upon the door or by a voice that will call 'Hurry up please
its time'. It is time that 'must have a stop'. The title of the third
section is sufficiently explained by Eliot's reference to Buddha
and Augustine. We have passed from 'the torment of love
unsatisfied' to the 'greater torment of love satisfied', from
sterility to barren lusts, mere 'affairs' of different kinds, fruit-
less, mechanical and meaningless. 'Death by Water' washes
our imaginations clean. Though the longing to expunge
memory and desire and to return to nothingness could not
give the poem its needed conclusion, this section acts like
a purification. As Phlebas passes the 'stages of his age and youth',
the past loses its power over him and the future no longer
demands calculation. He forgets the profit and the loss; and
when we come to the final section we have left London behind
us, left behind us the power of memory, left behind us the
anxiety for the future. We are wholly in a present in which
two things are demanded of us: patience and effort. London is
only one of the unreal cities we see over the mountains. No
persons pass before us in their habit as they live, only mysterious
figures, the 'hooded man' perhaps, but 'I do not know whether
a man or a woman'; and a woman in a nightmare vision who
fiddles on her long black hair. We are everywhere and
nowhere, and at one time and no time: at Jerusalem after the
entombment, making our way up a rocky mountain path,
on the road to Emmaus, or with explorers at the limit of their
endurance at the South Pole, at Biblis with the women
mourning the slain Adonis, or with Rachel mourning for
her children, or with refugees from the Russian and every
revolution, and from every city that has or will perish in violent
war, and in a deserted chapel among heaps of tumbled graves
in 'a decayed hole among the mountains' where the cock,
who is both Peter's cock of betrayal and the 'cock who is
the herald of the morn', crows, and finally by the banks of the
Ganges, where we hear the thunder speak. Its commands are
in a strange, ancient language, and alas, we need notes to tell
us what they mean, But Eliot could not have got his effect

otherwise. These commands are different from other commands in the poem. They come out of heaven, and thunder
in every mythology is always the voice of God. They are
strange and awe-inspiring. Familiar words from Scriptures we
know would not serve here. Words of immense, impersonal
authority are needed, which are not the poet's own. They
invade the poem. The replies to them are poignantly personal
and individual: but the voice of the thunder is something
different from the other voices that have echoed through the
poem, voices of sufferings, fears and desires, of guilt and disgust,
voices of thoughts churning round in the head, prophetic,
minatory voices. When the thunder speaks, it speaks to us
from without, demanding assent to its commands even though
they seem impossible of fulfilment.

The Waste Land does not end with affirmation. It ends with
a dismissive blessing—'Shantih shantih shantih': 'Peace, peace,
peace'—and not with the cry 'The horror! The horror!' of the
epigraph from Conrad which Eliot declared was 'somewhat
elucidative'. The peace invoked at the end as a blessing is the
peace that comes from discovery and acceptance of the truth in
all its horror: the truth of human failure and of human need.
It is a very different close from the close of the other great
work of the imagination whose jubilee we are celebrating this
year, and which profoundly influenced *The Waste Land*, James
Joyce's *Ulysses*. In these two great works the comic acceptance
of the conditions of life in this world and the tragic acceptance
confront each other. They each end by saying 'Yes'; but the
universes they accept are radically different: the one being
sufficient for man's need to love and to be loved, the other
insufficient, unless the rain, which we ourselves cannot
command, will fall.

The Adamson lectures

were founded in 1903 by friends and former colleagues of the late Professor Robert Adamson, who held the Chair of Logic at Owens College from 1876 to 1893.

1905 *Mechanism and morals* by Professor James Ward
1907 *The electrical basis of modern physical theories* by Sir J. J. Thomson
1909 *English poetry and German philosophy in the age of Wordsworth* by Professor A. C. Bradley
1910 *Leibnitz as a politician* by Sir A. W. Ward
1913 *The distinction between mind and its objects* by Bernard Bosanquet
1914 *Animal spirits* by Professor C. S. Sherrington
1919 *Satanism and the world order* by Professor Gilbert Murray
1921 *Relativity* by Albert Einstein
1923 *Reason and enthusiasm in the eighteenth century* by Professor Oliver Elton
1925 *Art and the material* by Honorary Professor Samuel Alexander
1927 *The mystery of time* by Professor A. S. Eddington
1930 *Carlyle and the hero* by Herbert J. C. Grierson
1932 *John Locke* by Professor N. Kemp Smith
1938 *Magnitude* by Sir D'Arcy W. Thompson
1947 *The classical background of English poetry* by Professor C. M. Bowra
1953 *Philosophical styles* by Professor Brand Blanshard